Lila's SUP Adventures

Once upon a time, there was a little girl named Lila who loved to explore...

One day, while walking along the beach with her parents, she saw some people standing on boards and paddling out to sea.

They looked like they were having so much fun!

Lila asked her parents what they were doing, and they told her that it was called stand-up paddleboarding, or SUP for short.

They explained that it was like surfing, but with a paddle to help you move and steer.

Lila was fascinated and begged her parents to let her try.

At first, they were hesitant, but they could see how excited she was, so they rented a board and a paddle for her.

Lila was a bit nervous at first, but she soon got the hang of it.

She paddled out to sea and felt the sun on her face and the wind in her hair.

She saw fish swimming below her and birds flying overhead. She felt free and happy.

But then, something unexpected happened. A sudden gust of wind blew her board off course and towards a rocky cove. !

Lila panicked and started to paddle frantically, but it was no use. She was headed straight for the rocks

Just when she thought she was going to crash, she heard a voice calling out to her.

It was a friendly seal who had been watching her from a distance.

The seal swam over and nudged her board away from the rocks.
Lila was grateful and amazed.

She realised that she wasn't alone out there and that the ocean was full of wonderful creatures who could help her if she needed it.

The Seal stayed with her till she was safe.

She paddled back to shore, feeling more confident and inspired than ever.

From that day on, Lila became a stand-up paddleboarding enthusiast.

She explored new beaches and coves, and she even made some new friends - including the seal who had saved her life.

The End

Lila will be back soon with lots of new adventures:

Lila joins a SUP group, learns to race and will continue her exploration of our oceans.

If your going on your own SUP Adventure, remebr thease 5 simple things to keep you safer:

Wear a Personal Flotation Device.

Carry a means of communication on you.

Check the Weather

Tell others of your plans

Paddle within your ability

We always advise you get some instruction before venturing out.

Coming Soon..

Lila's First SUP Race

Lila's Finds a Wreck

Lila and the Big Clean Up

Lila's Fist Multi Day SUP Adventure

Printed in Great Britain
by Amazon